Drawing Together to Build Character

Drawing Together to

Build Character

Written by Marge Eaton Heegaard

To be illustrated by children
to help families communicate and learn together

Fairview Press

Published by Fairview Press, 2450 Riverside Avenue, Minneapolis, Minnesota 55454. Fairview Press is a division of Fairview Health Services, a community-focused health system affiliated with the University of Minnesota and providing a complete range of services, from the prevention of illness and injury to care for the most complex medical conditions. For a free current catalog of Fairview Press titles, please call toll-free 1-800-544-8207. Or visit our Web site at http://www.fairviewpress.org.

First Printing: July 2004

Printed in the United States

09 08 07 06 05 04   7 6 5 4 3 2 1

Cover design by Laurie Ingram, http://www.laurieingramdesign.com
Interior by Dorie McClelland of Spring Book Design, http://www.springbookdesign.com

About this book

This book is designed for children ages five through twelve to illustrate with pictures they choose to draw. Younger children may need help understanding some of the words and concepts in the book, but do not offer too many suggestions. This is their book; let them make their own decisions about what to draw and write.

Give the child a small box of new crayons to illustrate the book. While many children enjoy drawing with markers, crayons often encourage greater self-expression. Older children may prefer to use colored pencils.

Younger children like to illustrate books, because images come more naturally to them than words. Older children are more comfortable expressing themselves verbally and may use words with their illustrations.

As you work through the book together, focus on ideas and expression rather than artistic technique. Do not try to protect the child from difficult feelings. As children learn to understand and express their feelings, they develop lifelong values and strength of character.

If a drawing reveals that the child has misunderstood something, correct that misunderstanding gently. Remember that what a child perceives to be real is as powerful to that child as any reality.

To encourage conversation, periodically invite the child to tell you more about his or her drawings. At the end of each section, you may want to tell the child something you have learned and ask the child to tell you something he or she has learned. When the book is completed, encourage the child to share his or her work with another adult for review and continued learning. Save the book as a keepsake of childhood memories.

Adults can help children build character

Drawing Together to Build Character uses the creative process to bring out the best in children. It teaches generosity, integrity, fairness, respect, self-esteem, and other values to prepare children for happy, productive lives.

Developing values and character may sound like hard work, but children learn best when they're having fun. Play is the work of childhood, so it's no surprise that artwork, games, and other creative outlets will increase children's communication skills and self-awareness.

You can help children build character by encouraging them to play, draw, write, and sing. But it's also important to model the values you hope to instill and provide opportunities for practice. For example, you can:

- Monitor your child's TV and movie viewing. Young children need help resisting bad influences.
- Give your child opportunities to help people in need. This will direct your child's natural tendency to show caring and kindness to others.
- Find peaceful ways to avoid and settle conflicts. Seek out solutions that are more creative than punishments or time-outs. Constantly teach respect for others.
- Encourage children to help with simple chores, and don't demand perfection. This builds responsibility, confidence, and self-esteem.
- Be honest. Don't overdo or give unwarranted praise. Children know when they do well. They don't like to be praised if they don't deserve it.
- Correct or compliment the behavior, not the child. This demonstrates respect and caring.

- When a child does something wrong, stop the behavior and explain the problem. Give an appropriate consequence and encourage the child to make amends.
- Help children learn from their mistakes. If we shame children or make them feel guilty, they may become resentful and develop low self-esteem.
- Avoid the word "should." "Should" often comes with a preaching tone, which is not an effective way to teach. Instead, give children choices. Encourage them to make choices that are just, generous, and caring.
- Foster your child's relationship with a loving higher power. Use your own religious or spiritual beliefs to nurture a sense of faith, gratitude, wonder, and security.

This book uses the art process to help children learn to:

To children

This is your book. You will make it different from all other books by drawing your own thoughts and feelings. You do not need any special skills to illustrate the pages. Just use lines, shapes, and colors to draw the pictures that come into your head as you read the words on each page.

Begin with the first page and do the pages in order. Ask an adult for help with words or pages you do not understand. When you have done a few pages, stop and share your work with an adult who cares about you.

I hope you will have fun with this book. You will learn some important things to help you feel good about yourself and the time you spend with others.

I care about others.

(Draw a picture of what you do to show you care.)

Caring means giving love and attention to people and things.

I have friends.

(Draw a picture of your friends.)

Friends are kind. They try not to say mean things to each other.

I share my things with friends. We know how to take turns.

(Draw a picture of some things that you share.)

Always treat others the way you would like to be treated.

I feel good when I help others.

(Draw a picture of yourself helping someone.)

Kind people think of the needs and feelings of others. They help people and animals who are unhappy or in trouble.

It isn't always easy to be kind, but I try not to say unkind things when I am angry.

(Draw a time when it was hard to be kind.)

Caring people talk to others in a way that helps, not hurts. When you care, you imagine what it feels like to be the other person.

When other children act shy or lonely, I invite them to play.

(Draw a time you played with someone who was shy or lonely.)

Think about how you would feel if you were them.

Learning good table manners can be fun. Some families will give points for good manners and take away points for bad manners. They decide how many points are needed for children to order dessert when eating out.

"Eat Neat" Points

Points are given for:

Using your napkin
Sitting nicely
Waiting to begin
Looking neat and clean
Using silverware correctly
Saying "please" and "thank you"
Other _____
Other _____

Points are taken away for:

Playing with food
Talking with a full mouth
Eating with fingers
Noisy eating
Other gross noises
Whining or fighting
Other _____
Other _____

It is important to practice manners so everyone can enjoy their meal together.

"Good manners" means showing respect for others.

(Check ✓ the things you do.)

____ I pay attention when someone talks to me.
____ I take turns talking.
____ I do not interrupt others.
____ I use my quiet voice indoors.
____ I try to make others feel welcome.
____ I say "please" and "thank you."
____ I say "you're welcome."
____ I try new foods when I am a guest.
____ I compliment others.
____ I take my hat off indoors.
____ I cover my sneezes and coughs.
____ I don't say everything I think.
____ I wear appropriate clothes.
____ I use proper words with adults.
____ I apologize when I am wrong.
____ Other _____
____ Other _____

People take time to buy me presents or make me things.

(Draw a favorite present someone gave you.)

Remember to send a nice thank-you note.

Sometimes others can be very rude.

(Draw something rude that someone did.)

You can be polite even when others are being rude.
Ignore their rude behavior.

I show respect to people who are older than me, like grandparents, teachers, and others.

(Draw a picture of someone you respect.)

Older people should be treated special. Showing respect tells people that you care about them.

Other people have things I like to play with.

(Draw something you like to borrow.)

Ask before you use something that does not belong to you. Treat other people's things with special care.

There was a time when someone made fun of my friend or tried to turn me against them.

(Draw a time you stood up for a friend.)

Loyalty means standing up for your friends and family.

I think before I make promises.

(Draw a promise you once made.)

If you are trustworthy, it means that others can count on you to keep promises and do what you say you will do.

When we are waiting for dinner and everyone is hungry, I can help in the kitchen.

(Draw what you can do.)

Everyone should try to be helpful. Don't wait to be asked. Offer to help.

I do my homework and get ready for school on time.

(Draw something that makes this difficult.)

If you are dependable, it means that others don't have to bug you to do what has to be done.

Some chores are no fun at all.

(Draw a chore that you do not like to do.)

Do what you have to do first, then you can do what you want to do.

Sometimes I tell a little white lie—or even a big lie—to avoid punishment.

(Draw something you once lied about.)

You must be honest if you want others to trust you.
It is hard to like people you cannot trust.

When I make a mistake, I can be honest about it and say "I am sorry." Then I can do something to make it better.

(Draw what you did to make up for a mistake.)

You can learn from mistakes!

I have something called a conscience. It is a quiet little voice inside me that tells me if I am doing right or wrong.

(Draw a time you listened to your conscience.)

Practice truth and honesty every day to build good character.

Some people keep the things they find, even if these things belong to others.

(Draw something you found. Write about what you did with it.)

If you find something, it is important to try to find the owner.

Some people try to cheat just to win a game.

(Draw how you would feel if that happened to you.)

Winning is not as important as others feelings good about you . . . and you feeling good about yourself.

I once did something that I knew was wrong. I thought it would make me feel good, but I felt bad.

(Draw what you did.)

Honesty brings good feelings. Being dishonest brings guilt and other difficult feelings.

My favorite games are . . .

(Draw your favorite games to play.)

Games can teach people to play fair and have fun,
whether they are winning or losing.

Some people boast when they win, or they complain and argue when they lose.

(Draw how someone you know acts.)

These people are not fun to play with. Do your best, but do not boast when you win or complain when you lose.

It is a lot of fun to play sports.

(Draw a picture about your favorite sport.)

Team sports can teach people to work together, play by the rules, and show good sportsmanship.

I feel frustrated when I want something right away and I have to wait.

(Draw a time you felt frustrated.)

Patience means waiting quietly without complaining.

There is something at home or school that does not seem fair.

(Draw a picture or write about it.)

Share your concerns with someone you trust.

Friends and family sometimes fight when they have to divide something evenly.

(Draw an example.)

Let one person do the dividing and let the other person choose first.

Sometimes I make a big mistake. I get so mad at myself!

(Draw a mistake you made.)

Everyone makes mistakes. If you forgive yourself and others, you can learn from mistakes and change for the better.

It can be hard to try new things, or to keep trying after I fail.

(Draw a time you failed at something.)

Courage means doing something difficult, even if you are afraid.

I was born with some special talents and abilities.

(Draw something you are good at.)

Gratitude means being thankful for what you have and for the world you live in.

There are many beautiful places in our world.

(Draw your favorite place in nature.)

Treat your world with care and respect to keep it clean and healthy.

When I am waiting for a meal or snack, I can think of poor people who are hungry and need many things.

(Draw some things people can give to the needy.)

We can all help those in need . . . and we must.

I give thanks every day for food, family, and other good things in my life.

(Draw or write what you do to show you are thankful.)

Celebrate the good things in your life.

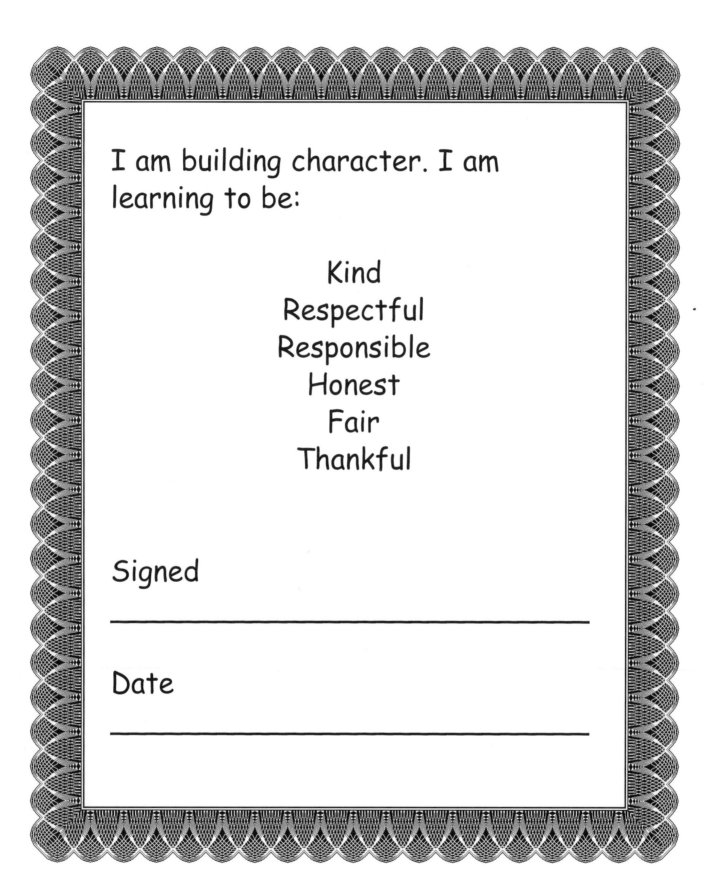

I am building character. I am learning to be:

Kind
Respectful
Responsible
Honest
Fair
Thankful

Signed

_____

Date

_____